my greenhouse

my greenhouse

POETRY

bella mayo

Andrews McMeel
PUBLISHING®

dedicated to

to all the girls who've fallen in love,
and had their hearts broken.
this,
sweet angels,
is for you.
this is for you to see
you're not alone,
to see
everyone laughs,
everyone cries,
everyone loves
and everyone lies,
but one day,
no matter how much it hurts,
you
must
rise.

and to love.
you are my worst fear,
my greatest dream,
what i look forward to,
and what i run from.
you make me feel every emotion,
you can change my mind in a heartbeat,
you make me
smile and scream,
yet
i always want you back.

so to you,
for making
every dream
somehow a reality,
i continue to believe in you,
because you,
love,
are always worth it.

and lastly, to my permanent greenhouse,
my beautiful forever garden,
my love and my husband,
jacob mayo.
you have grown far past every
weak and wilted flower written
about in this book and made
my life as beautiful as the
fields of wildflowers i've
always dreamed about.
no one compares to you.

my garden,

absolutely mesmerizing.
i come in,
i water you,
i shower you with light and sun
all of my days in order to grow you to your
   best you.
my greenhouse that never stops growing.
just like a real-life garden;
i could look at you
all
day
long.

chapter one

you hung
the moon

my masked boy

the sun
thinks i'm her muse.
the flowers
think i'm their home.
the man in the moon
thinks i'm his friend.
but the trees,
they know who i am,
and they lead
everyone who will one day break my heart
right to me,
disguising them as soulmates.

my new interest

i know a boy.
clueless and goofy,
handsome and kind.
and although everything in me wants to hold out
   for what i once had,
it's like the heavens know about this boy
and are walking my feet
right to his.

my darling

let your heart dream;
let your mind wonder
what it could be.
and sometimes,
just sometimes,
give a piece of your heart away.

my little in-between

i like you,
but i don't.
i shouldn't,
but i do.
a game of Ping-Pong between what is
    and what isn't.
it's a friendly game,
with a bit more to it.
it's not what you think,
but it's not what you don't.
what fun we're having in this little in-between.

my crush

there's so much more to know about you,
so much more to learn,
so much more to adore.
or at least it's fun to think so.

my metaphor

sunshine in my eyes,
poetry on my lips,
rainbows on my feet,
art in my hands,
and you on my mind.

my little flirt

falling for you has been fun.
little hand touches,
subtle comments,
accidental eye contact from across the room.
we've all had this a time or two,
but something about this one feels a bit different.
i've got a good feeling about you.

my love i'll never take for granted

it was all a moment,
you looking at me with that gorgeous face.
your smile was contagious.
i reached for my camera to snap a photo,
but i quickly realized
it was all a moment
i didn't want to ruin.
now,
this moment sits in my memory
for me to replay over and over again.
this moment
is all mine.
and i wouldn't have it any other way.

my galaxy boy

i looked up,
i saw the stars,
i thought of you.
i thought of all the nights,
all the things you said,
all the ways you made me feel.
all of the stars—i had them.
they were mine.
you hung the moon;
i held the stars.

my "anything for you" love

you sat with me and painted.
i watched as art
made art,
and my heart
was full.

my greatest surprise

i looked up,
and before i knew it, we were falling in love.
i was so focused on everything else
i didn't even see it.
i didn't have to try.
i didn't have to wait for you to call me back
   and wonder if this was what i wanted.
it just happened.
i just knew it was what i wanted without a
   thought in my mind.
you were unexpected
and quick.
but isn't that exactly how it's supposed to be?

chapter two

**you are
the sun**

my feeling

we were sitting on the beach,
i was there in my suit,
you in your trunks;
i looked across and i fell in love;
i looked across and i figured it out.
it was you.
it was always you.
you were the butterflies constantly spinning
    in my stomach;
you were the reason my heart was in my gut.
you were the feeling of electricity running
    through my bones.
you were the feeling of blood pumping through
    my veins.
i looked for you for so long,
but you were right there,
what felt like
the oxygen—in and out of my lungs.

my chaser

a pursuit,
you're on an immense pursuit of the sun.
you speak so highly of her.
you never seem to stop journeying toward her.
you love her in her entirety.
i should know,
how many times do i hear you say,
"you are the sun."

my dear companion

helpful and loyal,
loving and kind.
an adventure and a home.
a romance and a comedy,
a safe place and a new horizon.
my dear companion,
and my
pride
and
joy.

my dreamer

my beating heart,
my blooming thoughts,
hidden in you.

my curious one

like a light with a blanket thrown over it,
you slowly pulled that blanket back.
seeing more of all the light in me
each day.
you continued to fall deeper in love.
look at me now, baby;
i'm shining.

my sweet talker

you are exactly what i wanted,
and nothing what i expected.
you're quiet
and calm.
your words are sweet like honey,
yet they don't come often.
though somehow
i love you more
than my heart has the capacity for.

my stud

my head—over heels,
my heart—skipping a beat,
my mind—constantly running rampant.
this is how i feel when i'm in love.
this is how i feel when i'm with you.
i feel as though the rest of the world is spinning
    around us.
i feel as though i opened all the wrong doors,
but finally,
i opened the door that led to you,
the door that led to the rest of my life.

my prince

captivated.
the way you look at me like everything you've
    wanted you've got.
the way i'm giddy the whole three seconds
    between you getting out of the car to you
    opening my door.
the way you throw me over your shoulder like it's
    nothing, like you will carry me into forever.
i'm totally captivated.

my home base

the wildflowers sway in your direction,
the lilacs point your way,
no matter if i can see you or not,
i can always find a bloom that'll guide me to you.

my golden boy

you,
my love,
were a rough start,
but by God, i stuck with you.
i saw gold where no one else could.
i saw potential where no one else would.
you were a battle that turned to blessing.
a struggle that turned to a story.
promise that turned to purpose.

my breath of fresh air

your voice is like water and sun,
your voice
is my growth.
as i open my ears to you,
it's almost as if i'm placed
on top of the world.

my gift

to know you
is to love you.
and to love you
is an honor.

my garden boy

the way the trees dance in autumn,
the way i ask for flowers and you say, "got 'em."
the way the sun shines when you're in town,
the way i smile when you're around.
do you see the similarities?
it's like our love is a copycat of nature,
and nature is a beautiful thing.

my little traveler

my little traveler,
stay another day.
i trust the winds will sail you back when
  it's your time,
but for now,
let's race on the beach
without a dollar to our name.
let's get lost in our little game
we like to call love.
stay another day,
my little traveler.
don't listen to the winds.

my love

you're the reason i go to sleep late and wake
    up early.
you're the reason i run, jump,
and throw my hands in the air like wildflowers
    in the wind.
you're the reason i bloom.
you're the reason i chase the sun
and fall on the clouds like it's their job to
    catch me.
i would hate to meet me without you.

my muse

only poetry could attempt to explain to you
the depths of my love.

my lookout

like a mountain,
the more hills,
the higher i climb,
the better the view gets.

my boy who pays attention

i forget how much you notice.
i forget that your mind is like a recorder,
brimming with recordings of each little thing i do,
so when you speak about my charisma and spirit,
i'm not sure what you're talking about.
but you
explain in great detail the depths of your love
for the way i scrunch my nose when i'm
    complimented,
to the way i whisper "i love you" the same way
    every time.
how i jump in your arms running at full force,
you remember it all,
and i know when you see how chipper i get when
    you do,
you're recording this too.

my one and only

people often say,
"you make my world go round."
and as much as my semi-melancholic self hates
   to say it,
my quarter-blithe self understands what it means.
you make skating feel like floating,
you make walking feel like dancing,
you make running feel like freedom.
you make me love me too.

my simile

i breathe in the winds of his love,
almost as if my lungs depend on it.
i dance around on shifting ground,
almost as if my feet depend on it.
and i fall freely and unafraid,
almost as if my life depends on it.

my work of heart

you make me feel like i can write again.
if i have learned anything, it's that
it is not raw talent that pulls beautiful things out
   of thin air and puts them into words.
it's you.
you are the art,
and you are the words.
i'm the artist and the poet,
but you, my love, are my muse.

my potential heartbreaker

i think i love you more than i even know,
which is scary and lovely all at once.
life with you is the adventure of a lifetime,
but to lose you would be the loss of one.

my home

at first it was all about my heart beating fast
  when i saw you,
but now
if anything, my heart slows down,
because you,
my sweet home,
bring my heart peace,
a simple safety,
a sincere security.
i adore your
intentional,
elaborate
spirit.

my greatest privilege

the moment you are hurt by the hands of a man,
the thought of being in another's seems reckless.
to fully love you i had to unlearn
the idea i had so strongly held on to—
that in a man's arms is a dangerous place.
i often say being loved by you is my greatest
  privilege,
and i mean that when i say it
because the gentleness of your touch
and the safety of your arms are privileges
i don't take lightly
and will never
take for granted.

my paradox

you are the greatest complex i've ever known.
you teach me to slow down and speed up.
you push me toward patience and spontaneity.
you love me with kindness and with truth.
you kiss me gently and with passion.
where you are is vacation, and it's home.
you've turned my life into a paradox.
a paradox that is you.

my consistent love

love is choosing
and re-choosing.
it isn't about the feeling of happiness or joy.
it's about the everyday commitment to say i'm
    going to love you when the going gets hard.
it isn't about the feeling when we kiss
or the adventures we go on.
it's about the everyday choosing of your person.
love is choosing
and re-choosing.
and that is a beautiful thing.

my favorite kind of schooling

between you and me,
there is no algebra,
not even calculus.
just chemistry for the fiery moments of passion,
literature for the poetry of "i love you,"
and a whole lot of history.

my small-town boy

go buy her flowers or pick them from the side
   of the road.
go paint him a picture or write him a poem.
kiss her on the forehead,
take him around your hometown.
tell her you love her,
tell him you respect him.
make each other laugh, and hold one
   another's hands,
cook your favorite meal, and dance around
   the kitchen.
don't you see?
there's so much joy and beauty
only the simple can bring.

my love story

these days there's only so much you get to own in
   the world,
so many things you get to have to yourself.
that's why only you and i know our story.
we get to tell it to who we want,
when we want.
our story is ours to own.
so, baby,
i'm owning it.

my shape-shifter pt. 1

i wake up every day wondering which of you
   i'll get.
will i get my happy, bold, smiley boy
or my quiet, calm, loving one?
will i get my standoffish, mute, straight-faced boy
or my silly, singing, fun one?
i love every side of you.
even the ones that make me mad, i can't help
   but love.
you
are a mystery book
i can't stop reading.

my worrier

your biggest fear is hurting me in the end.
what do i have to do to help you understand
there doesn't have to be an end?

my sweetheart

meant to be.
could it be
that two could be
meant to be?
if all is meant to be, then where is the adventure,
the search,
the risk,
the choice?
do you choose to love me,
or is that just meant to be?

my pure love

i remember it.
where were we?
the beach, a parking lot, my house.
i remember it.
we were dancing,
you told me you get lost in my eyes.
you picked me up so strong.
i stepped on your toes,
butterfly kisses, nose to nose.
flowers on the counter i can see with sleepy eyes.
i remember it.
i wrapped my arms around your neck and tucked
    my head on your shoulder.
you kissed me on the forehead and said,
    "you know you'll see me soon,"
and i knew i wanted to remember it.
so that's what i did.
i remembered it.

my sweet reader pt. 1

i hope to paint a picture with my words,
like when i say,
"with spring in bloom,"
i hope you see the wildflowers that appear along
  the highway in early march.
when i say,
"wrapped in your arms,"
i hope you see your dreams,
when i say,
"my love,"
i hope you see the face of your own.
and most importantly,
when i say,
"i,"
i hope
you see you.

chapter three

neutral colors
and
dark clouds

my continual heartbreaker

sunrise—it's like we meet again for the first time.
breakfast rolls around and we fall right back
   in love,
afternoon—and we're on cloud nine, laughter
   and kisses.
evening comes and we're arguing about the
   smallest of issues.
yelling and screaming, anger and hurt.
by dinner, we don't even know how to talk to
   each other.
midnight—the moon is up,
and so are the stars.
i'm back in bed,
tears streaming down my face,
wondering how we fell this far,
i manage to fall asleep,
but hours later,
the sun rises,
and paralyzed by time,
we wake up
and do this all over again.

my storyteller

i sat there and listened
as you fed me beautiful lies.
i sat there in awe
as you poured out empty promises.
my eyes transfixed on the here and the now,
losing sight of what was really happening.
i was believing the fairy tale you were reading me,
while all along,
it was only a fairy tale.

my shape shifter pt. 2

you now
is nothing like the you i fell in love with.
i wouldn't fight for this you,
if i didn't know how good you could be.
the memories are what i cling to
when i just don't know why i'm still in this.

my inconsistent love

your inconsistency
is slowly killing me.
it's eating away at every last bit of my thoughts.
i can't sit at a stop sign peacefully anymore.
you've got every last bit of my mind.
i sit and wallow in my thoughts about if maybe,
just maybe, you will be in the mood and
    call me tonight.
this kind of love is not what i signed up for.

my indecisive one

i need you to make a choice;
you either stay
or you go.
you don't get to just have me when you want me;
not everything is on your terms.
no more MIA for three days,
then
when she's not responding,
you miss me.
i don't deserve that.
because if this is how someone treated my friend,
that would be exactly what i'd tell her—
you don't deserve that,
pretty girl.

my over-expectant love

you come and you go like you own the place.
wake up, baby,
this is my heart,
my mind,
my soul.
you don't own a thing.
all of this
convenient love
just isn't cutting it.
choose me
or lose me.

my two-faced boy

emotions vs. truth.
the truth is you were bad to me,
you hurt me,
you didn't keep a single promise,
yet my emotions swear you hung the moon.
they even believe you love me.
as the truth whispers what it knows,
my emotions scream what they feel.
the truth is peaceful, honest, and so loving.
my emotions are dramatic, wild, and obtrusive.
each fighting to be heard,
what feels good is wrong and what's right
  hurts worse.
what kind of messed-up game is this?

my boy with no feelings

i said there's no way.
there's no way
goodbye was that easy.
and in that moment i knew
nothing would ever be the same.

my blind side

the last time i kissed you,
i didn't know it would be just that.
my biggest fear was coming true
right before my eyes,
and i had
not one clue.

my deceiver

was i blind?
was i confused?
were we real?
i had this whole idea in my head.
i thought you did too.
i thought it was you and me.
did i dream all this up?
you've got me almost manic.

my charming boy

lost.
lost in your pretty little face that
no matter what draws me in,
no matter how many tears i shed the night before,
no matter the frustration,
no matter the shattered aching of my heart,
i remain lost in you.
something about you forces me to look
and draws me in.
lost in your
pretty little face.
lost in my
boundless love.
so,
so
lost.

my one i'm willing to work for

a heart breaks just like glass on a tile floor.
it's our job to decide
when we sweep it up.
do we throw it away
or try to glue it back together?

my forgetful one

falling in love is easy.
it's a feeling,
an uncontrolled and uncontainable feeling.
loving is a choice,
a challenging and conscious decision.
so before you say i just don't love you anymore,
remember that choice you used to make daily.

my hardest goodbye

you're the comic relief and the beautiful face,
the life of the party and the sweet words.
the only thing you're missing is the reliability.
you have all the tools to make me fall in love
    with you
but none of the ones to make me stay.

my straightforward love

a boy once told me,
   "you could be with someone a billion times
   better than me"
to which i replied,

"i don't want better,
i just want you."

foolishness.
looking back, i think,
"how do you not know you are better than that?"
but the truth of the matter is
that is what love does to you.
love makes you forget all the bad things.
when love feels threatened, it sends all of the
   sweetest memories
to the forefront of your mind
so that even if you wanted to,
even if you knew it was true,
you couldn't agree.

my childhood home

oblivion is like your childhood home.
it's your safest place,
but once you move,
you can't go back.

my boy with depth

i envy the storefronts that you look in,
because i know what it feels like when you like
   what you see.
you saw more to me.
in the moments we shared,
you saw right through my facade
into all the joy
and beauty
so
flawed.

my smart one

"i don't deserve you,"
you say.
you're right,
you don't.

my hurtful one

sometimes i think i'd rather be fighting than
  be this.
sometimes i think i'd rather be crying because of
  you than crying without you.
sometimes i even wish you were yelling at me
  again, because then at least i'd know i'm on
  your mind.
it's twisted, i know, but it's true.
it's the feeling of wanting the broken,
wanting everything to just go back to how it was.
at times it almost feels like the hour of laughter
  outweighs the twenty-three of tearful eyes.

my boy who's not all that

i laugh when people think
i have the perfect life,
the perfect face,
the perfect body
with the perfect friendships,
and of course,
the perfect boy.
little do they know
it's all so far from perfect.

.

my summer love

just a few months
that went by too quickly.
but enough love
to live off of
for
a
lifetime.

my greatest heartache

yep, i've dated the lover.
i've also dated the cheater,
the liar,
the obsessor,
the one with the cute face and no personality.
i've made my rounds.
but the one who hurt the most
had to be
the "let's just be friends."

my player

the sun comes up,
then so does the moon.
another sleepless night,
waiting on you.

my needy one

my whole heart was not enough;
you needed more.
i was just the one strong enough to realize
the more was not in me.

my one who keeps me guessing

the fall,
the love,
the ache,
the break,
though the worst of them all
must be the
wondering.

my lost boy

i must find you,
i love you too much
to watch you crumble.
i will keep my door open,
my table long,
and like i told you all those months ago,
i'll be waiting here,
arms wide open,
ready
for when you decide to
come
back
home.

my prideful boy

is it pride?
is it pride that's keeping you away?
because if so,
honey, you know better.
honey, you are better,
and just like honey,
you are so much sweeter.
so take your pride,
throw it out the door,
and remember why you loved me.

my boy i'll always be proud of

i meant every "i love you."
every one
every way
every time.
even the ones you never heard
i meant.

my lazy love

fighting for your attention i pause—
this isn't how it's supposed to be.
i would do anything to be with you at
　every moment,
shouldn't that be reciprocated?
you,
my love, are my most favorite thing.
but this battle—
you giving ten percent,
me giving ninety,
it can't last forever.
i'm growing tired.

my unreliable boy

where do we stand in the wondering?
where do we stand when i don't know if you're
  coming home or if you're just playing little
  games?
when do i get to say, "okay, enough"?
when do i get to call, "but you said forever"?
who do i get to run to when your love runs out?
who do i get to tell when you say it was all
  just a game?
what do i do when it's just me
left
with the wondering?
left
without.

my boy that broke me

i have yet to touch a paintbrush since you.
i can't bear the thought of what used to be pink
    balloons and sunny skies,
now neutral colors and dark clouds.
and although it's been months since i've slipped
    an apron over my messy hair,
i never stopped writing;
i promised you i wouldn't.
i promised you i'd write every day,
because it takes me away from the world.
i still write,
but from a different perspective,
heartbroken
and hopeful.

my broken self

i watch as people come and go,
i watch as they melt you and break you.
i watch as you take your time to heal only for this
    to happen over and over again,
then when i've had enough
i step back to see your face,
so i know whose heart i've been watching
    repeatedly shatter.
i turn the lights on and look up,
my breath swept away
to see the face
i was most worried i'd see,
my own.

my temporary love

don't make yourself too comfortable.
you're just here to make the days
a little more bearable
and my thoughts
a little more quiet.

my little heartbreaker

i run to you knowing your games,
i cry for you knowing you're okay,
i wait for you knowing you're free,
because, well—
well,
you're my little heartbreaker
i never want to get over.

my right person, wrong time

you will never hear me say, "i wish i never
   met you,"
although sometimes i feel that way.
i don't say it because it's not that i wish i never
   met you,
it's that i wish i could've met you later on down
   the road.
i'd do anything to meet future you.
i'd do anything to meet you once you've grown up
and realize what's important.
there's no one quite like you.
so—
i hope future you is single.

my home

i remember what it felt like to be wrapped in
  your arms,
i remember it exactly.
the feeling of safety, security, warmth.
the feeling of home.
hugging you was coming home.
nothing can replace my sweet and cozy home.

my boy who has me wrapped around his fingers

every "i love you" hung on my heart like flyers on
   a bulletin board,
one pinned on top of another
barely holding against the wind.

my boy i'm not quite over

the closer i get to closure,
the harder it gets.
don't you see,
i don't want closure?
i just want you.

my sweet reader pt. 2

if you've made it here
and my words are still my words to you,
you've missed the whole point.
you've missed the feeling.
let my heartache
help you understand your heartbreak.
let my love
write the story for your dreams.
let my words
be your words
when you don't know what to say.

chapter four

the tide
and
the moon

my most predictable love

right when another was about to catch my eye,
you came
just in time.
almost like you knew someone was about to take
  me away from all the hurt you caused and you
  decided who better for the job
than you.

my casanova

manipulation at its finest,
you know the game better than anyone i know.
you know the exact amount to give
to make me do the rest.
i wonder how many girls you've used this on.
i wonder how many girls you're using this on.
i'll give it to you though.
the way you look at me and ask the exact
   right questions
to make me fall on top of you
and still you have seemingly no part in it.
the way you get me to say i want you,
when i came to tell you i don't.
you are brilliant,
but i'm catching on.

my great mistake

the way you work is shameful.
the way you play me is sick.
the way my eyes are fixed on you is exhausting.
you're a mistake i can't stop making.

my true love

we don't stay far for long.
we should know by now,
no matter how many times we come apart,
we always come back.
we don't stay far for long.

my mysterious one

openhearted i am,
always wearing my heart on my sleeve.
but you,
my closed-hearted lover,
are the most intriguing human i've encountered.
you pull me in by pushing me away,
you grab me by letting go,
you have me
when you lose me.

my young love

my heart beating faster,
it's been so long since i've heard your voice
i almost forgot the effect it has on me.
the spontaneous acts it makes me do,
the heart-in-my-gut-feeling,
the uncontrollable
pain-in-the-jaw smile that melts in my face.
young and in love.

my on and off again

my stomach hurts just thinking about you.
oh the butterflies i missed
while we were "off again."

my reckless love

finally,
your long-awaited return.
i missed you more than the tide misses the moon,
but although the feelings are back and bright,
the question still remains—
this time,
will you stay?

my second chance

scared.
i'm scared to let you back in,
but i'm far more scared
to not.

my wildflower

you don't come back
till there's someone new.
like wildflowers in spring realizing
we're all happy the sun's come out
and so they must join.
and so
i must choose.
do i want the sun,
who rises in every season
and has never failed me?
or the wildflowers who come and go
without warning or explanation?
the wildflowers who may just be my favorite
   thing in the world
but will not stay through winter?
i must decide,
is the happiness you give me
worth the pain of knowing
in a few short months
you will wilt away
just
like
that?

my always and forever

you have given me a new hope,
a hope for a fresh start,
a hope for an all-new,
all-better us.
man, i hope you're serious,
because, baby, i'm ready,
ready to go all in.

my heart stealer

we're growing up,
meeting new people.
but i keep coming back to you,
almost as though my heartstrings are tied
   to yours
as tightly as a triple knot with a bow on top.

my great love

i get frustrated when you're not careful with
   my heart,
then i'm reminded
you don't even know you have it.

my soundtrack

you, my love, are like a song stuck in my head.
no matter how many more songs i listen to,
i still come back to you.
but you know what they say—
the only way to shake it
is to listen again.

my you

i'm
so
over
you.

until tomorrow.

my art

like art,
you're a masterpiece
of epic proportions.
like art,
you melt in my hands.
like art,
you take me to a place with no hurt
    or hard things.
and just like art,
you're always there
to pick up
right where we left off.

my ex

we can't be friends,
we can't even be acquaintances.
don't you see,
i'll fall right back in love with you?
you must remember,
we fall in love—
we do not to stay in it.

my no going back

who would've thought we would be here,
back again?
the only thing that didn't make it back with us
was the butterflies.

my former player

messing with my mind like you do,
thoughtless of what this would do to me
if this would make me hurt,
or this would make me heal.
makes me wonder,
were you always this thoughtless,
or am i just now seeing you differently?

my red x

you used to say i was toxic.
but, baby, i'm not toxic,
and maybe neither are you.
what's toxic is you and me together.
we are a compound science just won't allow.
a compound so toxic
it's almost lethal.

chapter five

you let go

my disrespectful love

it feels like an injustice,
an injustice to our relationship,
an injustice to our love,
an injustice to everything we once were,
for it to end
that easily,
that quickly,
no warning,
and seemingly no tears.
an injustice
would be an understatement.

my gone for good

gone.
just like that,
a part of my heart i never knew existed.
gone.
a part of my life i will never get back.
gone.
a part of my mind forever flooded.
just like that,
gone.

my master of manipulation

what you don't see is the way you cleverly found
    your way into each crack of my heart.
the way you intelligently wound your way into
    each corner of my mind.
the way you twisted my thoughts eight billion
    different ways until you got me where you
    wanted me.
you got me to believe it,
believe you'd never let go,
and just like that—
you
let
go.

my earthquake

"how are you?" everyone asks.
every part of me wants to say, "i'm so good!"
but i close my eyes
and in slow motion
i can see my tears,
i can hear my screams,
i can feel my shattered heart.
so i look up,
i shake my head.
i swallow my pride,
and i say,
"you know, i've been better."

my lifelong dream

i'm living my biggest nightmare,
and all i can think about
is when i had my arms
wrapped
around
my dream.

my secret heartbreaker

my happiest days to date were with him,
but don't let that fool you—
so were my worst.
romanticizing time like it's going out of style.
—
i think back to months ago
and i see our happy smiles,
i can hear our "i love you's,"
but what i seem to forget
is all the tears.
it's like my ears no longer remember the tone of
    your voice when you're mad.
all i remember is that laugh,
all i remember is "i love you,"
and that's why i write,
because you can't forget
what's written down on paper.

my miss you love

i used to drive and sit outside your high school
just because i missed you and wanted to feel close
   to you.
so imagine how i felt when you were gone
for good.
sad would be an understatement.

my charisma

i don't know what happened to me since you.
i don't show up,
i don't bring the party,
i don't smile as big.
maybe you were the party in me,
the big smile and the "i'm here, who's ready."
maybe that was never me in the first place.

my love that left me

the weeks following the end of our flame
were a blur.
i was never fully there,
and if my body was,
it's safe to say my mind wasn't.
everywhere i went, my head was somewhere else.
i could hear,
but i wasn't listening.
i could touch,
but i wasn't feeling.
i could watch,
but i wasn't seeing.
why is it fair that no one got all of me
because you wanted none of me?

my one who turned me dark

i looked in the mirror,
not shocked at the tearstains on my shirt,
not even sure what i looked like anymore without
   swollen eyes.
this was the moment i realized
sad had become the ordinary
and all else was merely the
exception.

my first heartbreak

when true love falls short,
when real love breaks easy,
when relentless love isn't so relentless,
will this be the ending to every story i will
    ever write?

my thoughtless love

how do you open your eyes in the morning and
   not think of me?
how do you hear that song and your eyes not fill
   with tears?
how do you eat there and not see me sitting right
   where i was, just weeks ago?
how do you talk to her, knowing she talks to me?
how do you do it?
was it hard for you to move on from me?
try moving on from you.
trust me—
it's worse.

my one great love

when i look at you,
i don't see all the bad.
i see all the smiles,
the closeness,
the "i love you's" and the "you're the bests,"
and now i know you were something special,
because when i look at him,
i can't even remember the good.
all i can see is the other girls,
the arguments and the tears,
the "i hate you's" and the "you're the worsts."
and that is how i know—
if there is such a thing as one great love,
you were mine.

my least favorite script

our story is a movie.
a watch-it-over-and-over-again
kind
of
movie.
a feel-every-emotion
kind
of
movie.
a tears-streaming-down-your-face-during-
the-credits
kind
of
movie.

my antagonist

i close my eyes because my mind is playing a film.
the opening scene pulls me in, as it shows you
    flashing that pretty little smile at me.
i laugh as it shows your eyes wandering around
    the room with the hope they don't somehow
    meet up with mine.
my heart races as i watch you throw me over your
    shoulder in the pouring rain and hurry me to
    the car.
but even though i know the ending, nothing
    prepares me for the final scene.
when you walk away for the very last time.
with swollen eyes, i try to remember every detail,
every muscle in your back,
every hair on your head.
i must remember
for times like this
when i forget how cruel the ending is
and i want to watch again.
i
must
remember.

my almost

had him and lost him.
so close yet so far.
so many sayings for when you're left in the dust.
you build up so much hype about "he's the
   perfect guy,"
then all of a sudden, what do you say?
well, maybe he is.
then why is he hers?
is he perfect,
just not perfect for me?
i don't know.
these things throw me.

my yesterday

"it'll get better,"
they say
time and time again,
but with each passing day,
my heart forgets why i must forget.

my one that ruined me

i force myself to write
on days like these
where not a creative bone in my body wants to
  think,
because they know whatever is coming is dark
  and wistful.
i force myself to write
when my mind is crying out for help
knowing the only one who can
is the girl staring back at me
when the screen goes dark.

my soft spot

i put up a tough front about him.
that whole "i couldn't care less about him"
    facade,
it's not real.
it just masks the fact that months have gone by,
    and i'm still not over him.
it just masks the fact that although he was awful
    to me,
passing by his house still ties a knot in my throat.
and though the world tells me i should've been
    over him months ago,
the smell of his cologne still burns.

my shocking loss

who have you become?
it feels like just yesterday
you were convincing me i was everything good in
    the world.
today i sit here in awe,
tears streaming down my face
wondering who the guy is sitting in front of me
telling me i'm just not good enough for him.
you fell so fast.
before this moment, i looked at you like you were
    the sun and the moon.
now,
you're nothing but another name
i'd be happy never hearing.

my overconfident one

do you ache in regret about the way you went
　　about losing me?
do you tremble in regret about how you loved me
so conveniently?
do you stop mid-sentence thinking about the way
　　you spoke to me?
or do you need a wake-up call?

my boy who left without closure

three months dreading even waking up.
two words i needed to hear.
one conversation that had to be.
as the words "i'm sorry" left your lips,
it was almost as though the ones that had
    haunted me for months,
"moving on,"
didn't scare me a bit.
it was the wildest feeling i've ever encountered.
in seconds,
just seconds,
a girl without hope
could
breathe
again.

my ironic one

"he's too good to be true,"
i said over and over again.
little did i know
i was so right.

my bug

my love bug stung me,
but time and time again i mistook it for a kiss.

my comeback boy

how brave it is to fall in love
knowing you're at risk of the hurting.
but far braver
is to fall in love again,
knowing the hurt and doing it anyway.

my happiest memory

after everything we've been through,
after every smile i smiled because of you,
after every tear i shed after you,
i still think about our love
as nothing less than my happiest memory.
though i step into tomorrow
believing for so much more.
believing for something that's mine.

my past life

you feel like another lifetime,
to merely think of you is an out-of-body
    experience.
me with you,
me without you—
two people i've known deeply.
although one keeps drifting further and
    further away,
between you and me,
i just can't keep up anymore.

my past

today.
today the sun rose and so did i.
something was special about today i didn't
    quite know.
i didn't know today would be the day
i came face-to-face with you,
and nothing hurt.
i was close enough to smell your cologne,
and it didn't burn.
today.
today i start all over.

the day has come,
to pack up my greenhouse and move on
   to the next.
the child in me kicking and screaming,
not quite ready to leave its home.
the mother in me, sad, but holding a smile,
knowing it's for the best.
and all of me,
grateful for the days of happiness
in my little sweet place
and equally grateful for the day's frustration.
as i box up all the sweetest memories,
as i box up all the growth
and leave behind all the pain,
i say,
"goodbye, my greenhouse,
it's time to plant somewhere new."

Bella Mayo is an actress and artist
from Louisiana. This is her first book.

First, thank you to the people who made this book come to life. Brandi and Allison, thank you for working alongside me to make this book what it is today. You guys have seriously made my dream come true. Thank you for allowing me creative freedom to share my heart as art.

Thank you to my parents and grandparents for pushing me my whole life to do everything for the love and good of others. To my Mom and my Twomama, you never taught me that I couldn't do what I set my mind to. For that, I am forever thankful.

Thank you to my siblings for loving me while all these stories were playing out. Thank you for the friendship you have provided me with my whole life. You guys have always been my biggest cheerleaders.

Thank you to my friends Kaylea, Ivy, Caziah, and Gabbie for giving up hours of your time to listen to me read these poems and ask for your opinions and advice.

Thank you to my friend and biggest helper, Lindsay, for making this possible for me. Nothing you do goes unnoticed. I couldn't have done it with you, I mean it.

Thank you to my husband, Jake, for encouraging me in my confidence as I share such a personal part of my story and supporting me in everything I do. I will love you forever.

Lastly, I want to say thank you to my fifteen-year-old self, who believed in herself enough to think that at her age, she could turn her journals into a poetry book. I also thank her for the countless nights of high school she spent at home with her hair up and glasses on, working to make this book not only beautiful but inspiring to anyone who picks it up.

Andrews McMeel Publishing
a division of Andrews McMeel Universal
1130 Walnut Street, Kansas City, Missouri 64106

www.andrewsmcmeel.com

22 23 24 25 26 RR4 10 9 8 7 6 5 4 3 2

ISBN: 978-1-5248-6285-5

Library of Congress Control Number: 2021934755

Editor: Allison Adler
Art Director: Julie Barnes
Production Editor: Jasmine Lim
Production Manager: Carol Coe

ATTENTION: SCHOOLS AND BUSINESSES
Andrews McMeel books are available at quantity
discounts with bulk purchase for educational, business,
or sales promotional use. For information, please
e-mail the Andrews McMeel Publishing Special Sales
Department: specialsales@amuniversal.com.